Frugal Seeds: 501 Ways to Make Save or Stretch a Dollar by Charlie Lee Austin

Published by:
Asynchronous Threads, LLC
345 Carlisle Street #1106
Mooresville, IN 46158

© 2019 Asynchronous Threads, LLC

All rights reserved. No portion of this book may be reproduced in any form without permission from the publisher, except as permitted by U.S. copyright law. For permissions contact:

info@AsynchronousThreads.com

ISBN 9781798662571

Dedication

We would like to thank God our Father for blessing us throughout our money-saving, frugal-living, debt-free journey.

As we walk this frugal path we are thankful for His mercy and grace.

We are also thankful for the children He has blessed us with, R, E, A, and KJ and their willingness to be a part of our frugal adventures. We appreciate your love and support and we are blessed beyond measure to be your parents.

Introduction

Welcome, dear reader.

I am so happy you are here.

The book you are about to read catalogues a number of things my husband and I have employed over the years to help us work toward our goals of eliminating our debt, saving for a dignified retirement, and having a little extra to enjoy life while our wonderful children are still at home.

While we are not yet out of the woods with regard to debt, only part of the mortgage is left and we have a much brighter outlook on the future. Not every suggestion shared here will necessarily fit your circumstances or lifestyle, but we sincerely hope that each one will be, if not directly useful, an inspiration to spark ideas to help you down the path of your own journey.

Paying off debt and saving money is hard work, but I know you can do it.

Blessings,

Charlie

Please know we are not responsible for the accuracy of websites. At the time of publication of this book we did our best to make sure all links provided accurate information.

Also, please note that any recipes found in this work are presented for entertainment and/or informational purposes. It is your responsibility to review the suggested ingredients carefully before use to ensure that they will not cause any adverse reaction for yourself, or for others with whom you might share the results of those recipes, whatever the intended use.

Frugal Seeds

501 Ways to Make Save or Stretch a Dollar

by
Charlie Lee Austin

A penny saved is a penny earned.

- *Benjamin Franklin*

1. Coupons are a great way to save money on stuff you're already planning to buy, and your local Sunday paper is probably full of them. Our local dollar store sells them for (wait for it) a dollar, which is a great savings off the newsstand pArice as well as the regular subscription price. Another benefit of buying this way is that you can get multiple copies if the coupons are particularly good for you, though some stores limit quantities. There are also several websites, including grocery-coupons-guid.com, that will let you know what coupons to expect before you spend gas getting to the store. Before you buy, be sure that the coupons are actually in the paper as they do go missing from time to time.

2. Quit smoking. This will not only give you the immediate savings from not buying tobacco, but can save you tons of money in health care costs over the years. Also, many employers now have monetary incentives for quitting.

3. Movie night doesn't have to cost an arm and a leg. Rather than going to the theater or even a video store, you can once again make use of the library. If the movie you're hoping to watch isn't in, you can always rent another and ask your library staff to put a hold on the title you want for next time.

4. If your library does not have the media items that you are looking for, check to see if they participate in interlibrary loans. This allows you to request items that are available at participating libraries which can be sent to your branch for you to check out.

5. If you prefer audiobooks, your library is once again likely to be a resource for savings. Many libraries offer not only books on CD but Playaways, which are digital audio players preloaded with audiobooks. They are small, lightweight, battery operated, and work with standard earbuds or headphones.

6. If you have an Amazon Prime membership, their music and movie streaming services are included. Prime Music gives you access to millions of songs from every genre available as well as the contents of any music you may have purchased on Amazon over the years. Prime Video gives you access to numerous movies and TV shows, as well as Amazon's original programming, 2 day or sooner free shipping on Amazon sold products, Whole Food benefits, unlimited cloud storage for photos, free e-books, 6 month digital subscription to Washington Post, free games, free audiobooks and even more.

7. If you like streaming video services such as Netflix, take advantage of their subscription flexibility. For instance, if you save 1 dollar a month for a year, you will have enough money, with a little left over, to pay for a Netflix subscription for one month, allowing you to binge watch all the movies you want to see for 30 days. There are several websites, including, digitaltrends.com, that list upcoming releases to help you plan the best month for you.

8. Save seeds from your garden to plant the following year. Choosing self-pollinating plants such as beans, peas, tomatoes and peppers works the best. Be sure to only save seeds from healthy plants. Take seeds from the mature plant or its fruit, rinse the seeds, lay them on waxed paper and leave them out for a week or two until seeds are completely dry. Once dry, place your seeds in an airtight container and store them in a cool dark place until next year. I have found seedsavers.org to be a great website for more detailed information.

9. Choose perennial plants and flowers such as asters, daisies, clematis, hostas, and trillium for your landscaping so they will return year after year.

10. Many plants and flowers, including hostas, daisies, black eyed susans, irises, daylilies and purple coneflowers can be easily split and replanted, stretching your landscaping budget. Better Homes and Gardens website, bhg.com, has a lot of great information on this topic.

11. Many libraries participate in the *My Library Rewards* program which you can find at mylibraryrewards.com. Signing up for the rewards program allows you to earn points for each item you check out. You can then redeem earned points for free or discounted foods, services, or tickets to local attractions in your area.

12. Sign up for Friday freebies available at many grocery stores. Some stores with such a program are Baker's City Market, Dillions, Food 4 Less, Food Co, Fred Meyer, Fry's, Gerbes, Jay C, King Soopers, Kroger, Owen's, Pay Less Supermarkets, Quality Food Center, Ralph's, and Smith's. This usually requires signing up for a store's discount card and downloading the freebie onto the card or app each week.

13. Sign up for the rewards programs for stores that you shop at regularly. These cards may allow you to virtually clip coupons to use in the store on your next visit and may come with a monetary reward for spending over a certain amount of money.

14. If you are going to eat out, make sure you first look for online coupons at restaurant.com, groupon.com and/or the restaurant's website.

15. Always go through the coupon packet that is delivered to your mailbox monthly by Valpak. There are usually coupons ranging from oil changes to restaurants and HVAC discounts to dental work.

16. Many fast food restaurants now have free apps that give you discounts and/or free food items. Some of the restaurants with apps include McDonald's, Chick-fil-A, Burger King, Jamba Juice, TCBY, Auntie Anne's, and Sonic. If you have a smart

phone, it's definitely worth taking a few minutes to see whether your favorite places offer such an app.

17. Eat as healthfully as possible so you can be sure to feel your best, maximize energy, and minimize visits to the doctor.

18. Challenge yourself to drink only water for a minimum of one week. If this sounds too daunting, infuse lemons, limes, berries or mint into your water for variety. Once you've completed your challenge check to see how much money you've saved and see how much better you feel.

19. Get your water tested. Most health departments or county soil and water departments offer free or low cost testing. This is especially important if you are on a well. This can save you a lot of money on health in the future.

20. Allow your municipal water to sit in a container without a lid for 24 hours to let it off gas before drinking. This will work if it your water is treated with chlorine but not chloramine. Off gassing will not only make your water taste better – encouraging you to drink more – but it will also be better for your health.

21. Save brown packing paper from deliveries to use for your own shipping or packing needs.

22. Shipping paper is also perfect for kids to decorate and then use as wrapping paper for gifts.

23. Use your kids' excess art work as wrapping paper for family gifts.

24. You can also use your children's art work as gifts for close family members. Frames can be purchased at a dollar store to create a personal gift that grandparents and others will cherish.

25. Cut up panels of cardboard boxes are perfect to line the bottom of chicken coops and cages for small animals like rats, gerbils, mice, bunnies, and chinchillas making life easier at cleaning time.

26. Avoid waste by melting broken crayons together to make a very special art utensil. Remove the paper, place the crayon pieces in a microwave-safe bowl and heat them up, stirring regularly. Pour the completely melted wax into a silicone mold. Once cool, pop the new crayon out of the mold and begin creating.

27. Make playdough from items around your house using the following recipe:

- 2 cups of flour
- 3/4 cups of salt
- 4 teaspoons of cream of tartar
- 2 cups of warm water
- 2 tablespoons of vegetable oil

Place the ingredients into a pot on the stove; stir over medium heat continuously until thick. Pour onto wax paper and let it cool. Knead until smooth. The dough can then be divided and tinted with a few drops of food coloring. You can also add glitter to make it more festive.

28. Save all scrap paper and printing mistakes for kids' craft projects. Keep it in a single location so children know where to find it.

29. Cut up scrap paper into equal sizes and place into a box or other container and use for jotting down notes.

30. Small to medium shipping, cereal, food, and shoe boxes can be taped shut to create wonderful blocks for kids to play with.

31. Large appliance boxes make one of the best kids' toys as they can be turned into a train, a car, an airplane, a castle, a bus, a

house, a church, or anything else their little imaginations can dream up.

32. Place your small pieces of soap into a mesh produce bag. Once you've gathered enough, it can be used to scrub your hands when they are really dirty.

33. If you have a Bank of America, Merrill Lynch, or U.S. Trust credit or debit card and a photo ID you can get a free general admission to participating museums the first full weekend of every month. Check out the card issuer's website to find participating museums near you or your planned vacation destination.

34. If you have clothing, sheets, or towels that aren't in good enough condition to donate, cut them into rags. Use these instead of paper towels.

35. Whenever possible, wash laundry in cold water and on the shortest cycle needed to get your clothing clean. This will save on energy costs.

36. Use only 3/4 of the laundry detergent suggested; it is usually more than enough to clean your clothing.

37. Some grocery stores give you points or money off your bill for bringing your own bags. Keep bags in your vehicle so you can take advantage of such discounts. I was able to purchase several large and sturdy reusable bags from our local farm store for 99 cents each and they have been invaluable for transporting groceries.

38. Use plastic grocery bags to line small trash cans.

39. Use plastic bread or grocery bags to pick up animal waste while on walks or even in your backyard.

40. Compost yard waste like grass clippings and leaves and use the rich soil in your garden or flower beds.

41. Spray vinegar on weeds to kill them. Vinegar will kill any plant it touches so make sure you only get the weed. It is perfect for unwanted plants in the cracks of your driveway or sidewalk.

42. Make sure all ceiling fans are rotating in the proper direction for the season. The fan should be rotating clockwise in the winter and counter clockwise in the summer for proper HVAC assistance.

43. When you can't squeeze any more toothpaste out of the tube, cut open the end; there's usually enough left for one or two more applications.

44. Add water to shampoo and conditioner when the bottle is nearly empty. Vigorously shake the bottle, this will allow you to get at least one more use out of it.

45. Use 1/2 the recommended amount of shampoo, it is more than enough to clean your hair.

46. Out of shampoo and conditioner? Pure lemon juice or apple cider vinegar can be used as shampoo. Hair conditioner alternatives include eggs, coconut oil and honey, aloe vera, yogurt, and hand lotion; just be sure to rinse your hair completely.

47. Freeze fruit before it goes bad. Frozen lemon, lime, or orange slices can be added to water for flavoring. Other fruits can be cut it up into smaller pieces and frozen for smoothies.

48. Freeze excess fresh herbs in ice cubes and save in freezer bags to be used in soups and stews.

49. Sell all unwanted media (vinyl records, CDs, DVDs, video games, blu-ray, audiobooks, playaways, magazines and books) to a used bookstore. Some used book stores will even purchase board games and electronic devices if they are in good condition.

50. Sign up for gas station rewards and remember to scan the card each visit. This can earn you money off each gallon, free gas, and free or discounted food and beverages.

51. Keep a small dry erase board on the fridge to write down all the leftovers that are hiding inside. Make sure everyone knows to mark things off as they are eaten and to add new items that are placed inside.

52. If you are able, cook double recipes; one for now and one for the freezer. When you are short on time you'll have a meal waiting and be less tempted to eat out.

53. Keep a master list of all prepared meals that are in the freezer. Make sure to keep it updated.

54. Save sturdy takeout food containers to be reused for leftovers, picnics, and lunches for work or school.

55. Save wide mouth glass salsa or queso jars and their lids to store leftovers; the clear glass makes it easy to see what is inside.

56. Save dryer lint from cotton clothing to make fire starters using the following method:

- Fill each section of a cardboard egg carton with lint
- pour candle wax over lint in each compartment (wax can be melted from old candles in a double boiler)
- let cool completely and cut apart cups

57. Home baked muffins are much cheaper than store bought. Tweak the muffin recipe below to suit your taste or dietary needs. You can easily swap in gluten free mixes, almond flour, non-dairy milk, and various oils. Note that each variation will change the taste and possibly the texture, so you'll want to experiment to find the combinations that work best for you.

Ingredients:

- 2 cups of flour
- 1 cup milk (any type)
- 1/2 cup of sugar - if using liquid sweetener decrease milk to 3/4 cup
- 2 teaspoon of baking powder
- 1/2 teaspoon of salt (optional)

- 1 teaspoon of cinnamon (if desired)
- 1 large egg
- 1/4 cup of oil
- 2 teaspoons of vanilla

Mix wet and dry ingredients separately and then add wet to dry. Mix until combined; it will be lumpy. Pour into muffin cups, makes approximately 12 regular sized muffins. Bake in a preheated oven at 400 degrees for approximately 20 minutes.

58. Save bones from fish, beef, chicken, and turkey to make stock.

Ingredients:

- 2-4 pounds of bones of the same type
- celery stalks
- carrots
- onions cut in half or quartered
- garlic cloves
- peppercorns
- water to cover

Simmer covered for several hours then let cool. Pour stock through cheese cloth and put in refrigerator overnight. In the morning, skim the fat off the top and discard. Broth should be used within a day or two or frozen to use at a later date.

59. Making granola at home is so much cheaper than purchasing it in a store.

Have fun experimenting with different ingredients in the following recipe:

- 5 cups of rolled oats (not quick oats)
- 1/3 cup vegetable oil
- 1/3 cup honey
- 3/4 cup brown sugar
- 3/4 cup shredded coconut
- 1 cup sliced/slivered nuts
- 1 cup raisins
- 1/2 teaspoon salt
- 1 tablespoon cinnamon
- 1 tablespoon vanilla

Mix brown sugar, oil, honey and vanilla in a saucepan over medium heat. Stir until sugar is dissolved. Mix all dry ingredients in a cake pan and pour sugar mixture over the dry ingredients. Bake at 350 degrees Fahrenheit for approximately 15-25 minutes, stirring ingredients every five minutes. Let cool; add raisins and store in an air tight container.

60. Create your drinks at home. Invest in good travel mugs and bottles to transport coffee, tea, smoothies, or infused water. This will save you a bunch of money in the long run, not just on the cost of drinks out but also in time and gas wasted waiting in a drive thru.

61. Use drive time productively; listen to audiobooks from the library and learn something new for free.

62. Need a tutor for you or your teenager? Many colleges offer free tutoring or an 800 help line for students in various subjects. Rose-Hulman offers free math and science help for students in grades 6 - 12 at 877-ASK-ROSE.

63. Do you have poster board that is only used on one side? You can cut it up to make flash cards or recipe cards or use the clean side for another kid's school project.

64. Declutter your entire living space. You could find things you forgot you had and avoid buying duplicates. My favorite decluttering book is Clutter's Last Stand by Don Aslett.

65. If you find you have things you don't need during your

whole house decluttering, you can make extra cash by selling those items at a garage sale, on eBay, or at a local consignment shop.

66. Pay all bills on time. If using the mail, allow enough time for delivery to avoid late charges. Late fees on credit cards can be up to 35 dollars. If you receive a late fee after a long record of paying on time, making a call to see if the fee can be waived is worth the effort.

67. If you can't pay a bill (or three) on time, call each company you owe before the bill is due to see if they can help with payment arrangements.

68. In most states you can call 211 to find available resources including food, shelter, clothing, childcare, and mental health assistance.

69. Save bags found inside cereal boxes to cut up into sheets and use like wax paper.

70. Medical bills tend to be sent to collections quickly. Make sure to call the billing department immediately to set up a payment plan if the bill cannot be paid in full.

71. When calling about billing issues, always write down the date, time, reason for your call, resolution (if there was one) and the name of the person with whom you spoke in case there is a further issue with the bill. This is especially important if a fee is being waved, interest rate or monthly cost is being reduced, or a payment plan is being implemented.

72. When dealing with the IRS, always send correspondence by Certified Mail with Return Receipt. Even though this costs money, in the long run it could save you lots of time, further headaches and, ultimately, money. Make sure you keep copies of everything you send, and be sure to file them with the related Return Receipt.

73. Plan your next family visit to one of our National Parks using https://www.nps.gov/planyourvisit/fee-free-parks.htm to take advantage of the several fee free admittance days offered every year.

74. Start a frugal book club. Books that could be used include three of my favorites: "The Complete Tightwad Gazette" by Amy Dacyczyn; "Your Money or Your Life: 9 Steps to Transforming Your Relationship with Money and Achieving Financial Independence: Fully Revised and Updated for 2018" by Vicki Robin and Joe Dominguez; and "Little House Living: The Make-Your-Own Guide to a Frugal, Simple, Self-Sufficient Life"

by Merissa A. Alink.

75. Have a clothing, book, toy and anything-you-are-no-longer-using exchange with your friends, family, or house of worship with everything free. All left overs can be donated to a local charity.

76. Set up a free table at your house of worship, work, or other organization allowing people to leave items they no longer need or want. Items can include everything from clothing to non-perishable food.

77. Research what free services are available from your local library. My small Midwest library offers the following items and services at no charge:

- notary
- faxing
- in-house tablet use
- private rooms for meetings or homework
- genealogy assistance
- museum passes
- computer classes
- story times

- book clubs
- knitting classes
- volunteer opportunities
- Wi-Fi hotspots
- board games
- cookie cutters
- baking pans
- and, of course, CDs, books, DVDs, magazines, newspapers, e-books, video games, audiobooks and playaways

78. Put dish soap in a hand soap pump for better portion control.

79. Do not use the drying setting on the dishwasher unless it is absolutely necessary.

80. Use the shortest dishwasher cycle that will effectively clean the dishes.

81. Utilize vet clinics at pet or farm supply stores and humane societies for low-cost shots and basic vet care for your pet.

82. Attend free health fairs at local hospitals and organizations and participate in the free screenings.

83. Use big box and discount stores' optical and pharmacy departments; most can be used without a membership and offer very competitive prices.

84. If you absolutely cannot pay for glasses check out respectacle.org for assistance.

85. Always turn off the lights, TV, and radio when you leave any room.

86. Keep lights and TVs on timers when you leave for an extended period of time; this is much cheaper and less hassle than dealing with a possible break in.

87. Purchase new clothing off season. Back-to-school time is when all the summer clothing is deeply discounted to make room for winter stuff. Around spring break is when you will begin to find winter clothes on sale. It can be very tempting to go overboard when prices are so low, so make sure to purchase only what is needed.

88. If you find discounted clothing or shoes that fit well,

purchase multiples if you're able, so you have another one when the first one wears out.

89. Store outgrown children's' clothing in clear plastic tubs labeled with sizes so they'll be easy to find for the next child.

90. Save cotton from the tops of medicine and vitamin bottles to be used for crafts, removing make-up and nail polish, making fire starters, and freshening a room by putting some drops of essential oil on the cotton and setting it out.

91. Save unmatched socks to make puppets for a child, cut into strips to tie up garden plants, or safely store holiday glassware in when not in use.

92. You can use your lonely cotton socks to make desiccants for your home. Simply fill the sock with silica gel beads from kitty litter or another source, tie the open end closed, and hang in any damp area. You could also use the silica beads to fill a plastic food container with a lid. Just put the beads in the container and punch several holes in the lid. You can find instructions for recharging silica gel online so you can get lots of reuse out of your homemade moisture absorbers.

93. Save coffee grounds to put around plants and trees that love

acidic soil such as evergreens, lilies, blueberries, hydrangeas, azaleas, huckleberry and holly bushes.

94. Use plastic storage drawers made for the garage as dressers for children. These hold up to kids' rough handling and have deep, easy-to-open drawers. Once the kids outgrow these, they'll have a new life as seasonal storage in the basement or attic, or doing heavy duty in the garage.

95. Use old t-shirts as bibs. Simply cut the shirt straight down the back and put your child's arms through and the sleeves and they will be completely covered.

96. Don't buy books, check them out. Your local library probably has a wider selection (though fewer copies) than your local book store and, you're likely already paying for it through property taxes anyway, even if you rent. One notable exception would be books you want to make notes in or refer to often, like this one.

97. Research all benefits that your employer offers. Some offer wholesale club memberships, discounts for numerous products and services, tuition reimbursement, and even commuter benefits for expenses like parking and mass transit.

98. Create a spa day at home for free. Take a long bubble bath complete with calming music and candles. Do your own manicure, pedicure and facial.

99. Take care of any leak in your house immediately, before it becomes a much bigger and more expensive problem.

100. Open window coverings in the winter to let the sun in and add warmth to your home and close them in the summer to keep the sunlight from warming up the house.

101. Use glass food jars as drinking glasses.

102. If the temperature and humidity drop enough on a summer evening open the windows, but remember to close them early in morning before it starts to heat back up.

103. Don't allow people to bully you into taking less than what you want for items you are selling. If you are asking a reasonable price, be patient it will sell.

104. Thinking about college? Check out your local community college; tuition is often much cheaper and most classes will transfer to many four-year schools.

105. Buy next year's Christmas wrapping paper during after-Christmas sales for some huge discounts.

106. Buy candy after Halloween, when it is greatly discounted, to use for Christmas. Some candies, while bulk-packaged and marketed for Halloween, have plain individual wrappers making them useful well after that spooky night.

107. Every trip to the grocery store, purchase a few extra non-perishable items that you would normally use and build up your pantry. A pantry can be very beneficial to have when times get tougher. Make sure to rotate food from your pantry into everyday meal planning.

108. Whenever practical, keep your home's interior doors open to allow maximum air transfer for heating and cooling.

109. Don't buy shelving to create your new pantry. Use space you already have such as under your bed or stairs, a cleared bookcase, or a few shelves in a closet.

110. Save all your pocket change in a large repurposed container. Many banks and credit unions offer free coin-to-cash

service if you are a member. Just make sure to have a plan for the money, such as putting it towards a specific bill you are working hard to pay off, before taking it in.

111. Go to myfridgefood.com for recipe suggestions based on the food you already have in your home.

112. Food grade buckets can be found free for the asking at many grocery store deli departments and are great for storing your bulk dry goods.

113. Store plastic grocery bags in an empty tissue box near the door so you can easily grab a few on the way out to walk your dog or to clean out your car.

114. Poison control is a free and confidential call staffed 24/7 by nurses, pharmacists, and doctors with special training in toxicology and managing poisonings. They are available any time to help answer your questions and to recommend the best next steps if someone has been exposed to a potentially toxic product, poison, or medication, and it could help you avoid an unnecessary trip to the ER. 1-800-222-1222 or visit PoisonHelp.org

115. Keep a journal to write down every penny you spend in an

entire month. This is a great way to see where you may be able to reign in some of your spending.

116. Pick one or two months out of the year to go on a spending fast, buying the absolute minimum necessary. Some suggestions: try to limit your meals to what you already have on hand, dump Netflix for the month, make your coffee at home, and only leave the house when required. Use your savings to retire debt or put away for longer term goals.

117. Learn to do simple vehicle maintenance yourself; YouTube is a great resource as is repairpal.com.

118. Tackle as many home repair and maintenance tasks as you feel comfortable with on your own. Once again, YouTube is a great resource, and can help you gain confidence and steadily expand your skillset. Create and post a schedule of required regular maintenance.

119. Always search for coupon codes before purchasing anything online. There are many websites that list available codes including retailmenot.com.

120. Visit freebie sites such as vonbeau.com or sweetfreestuff.com to find freebies that might be helpful to you.

121. Maintain a running list of groceries you need and post it on your refrigerator; make sure to take it with you when you go to the store and purchase only what's on the list.

122. Governments at various levels and many local charities offer free summer meals for all kids 18 and under. Meals are typically available Monday through Friday throughout the summer at locations such as city parks and public schools. Visit http://fns.usda.gov/sfsp/summer-food-service-program to find many of the available summer meal programs. Location updates usually start to appear in the month of May.

123. Take advantage of free summer reading programs available at most local libraries and book stores, such as Barnes & Noble and Half Price Books, as well as some theaters including Cinema de Lux, Showcase, and Multiplex Cinemas.

124. Leave your oven door open after food is done cooking to get a quick boost of warmth in the winter.

125. Instead of purchasing individual snack bags, buy the party-size bag and store the contents in individual zipper bags.

126. Many bowling alleys offer free bowling for kids all summer long. Check out kidsbowlfree.com for more information.

127. Many movie theaters offer free or discounted daytime showings for kids during summer. Some participating cinemas include Regal theaters, Goodrich Quality Theaters, and Marquee Cinemas; be sure to check with your local theater.

128. Download or print free books from the following sites:

- Guttenburg.org
- OpenLibrary.org
- Bookboon.com
- Archive.org
- Feedbooks.com
- en.childrenslibrary.org
- pdfbooksworld.com
- FreeComputerBooks.com
- Questia.com/library
- Authorama.com
- ManyBooks.net
- en.WikiBooks.org

- Sacred-texts.com
- onlinebooks.library.upenn.edu
- FullBooks.com

129. Be sure you're getting the best price for your groceries by comparing the price per unit. Walmart and other stores make this easier by providing the price per ounce or per count on the shelf label. You'll be surprised just how often the bigger "bulk" package costs more per unit.

130. If you are in need of food, consider going to a local food pantry. Check out local churches and organizations; many will have a sign in front of their building listing dates and times the pantry is open. Check sites like feedingamerica.org and littlefreepantry.org to see what resources are available near you.

131. Send postcards instead of greeting cards to save money on postage.

132. Cut off the front of clean greeting cards and use as postcards.

133. Save all free greeting cards sent to you in the mail; don't feel guilty for using them.

134. If you need to purchase greeting cards, many Dollar Tree stores now offer Hallmark cards.

135. Shop at discount grocery or salvage stores that specialize in damaged or past date foods. You can save a lot of money and they tend to offer higher-end products.

136. Need a quick deicer for your windshield and locks? Mix 1 part isopropyl alcohol and 1 part water in a plastic spray bottle and spray liberally on the windshield. Turn on your wipers to clear the glass. If your locks are frozen, spray a stream into the lock; wait a moment before inserting the key.

137. Take snacks and drinks with you when you run errands so you're not tempted to hit the drive thru when everyone is tired and hungry.

138. Keep a bag of clay kitty litter and some cardboard in your vehicle during the cold weather months in case you need more traction to get going. This can prevent an expensive tow.

139. Save money when camping by searching freecampsites.net.

140. Take a moment before leaving the house to think whether there are errands that make sense to bundle into the same trip.

141. Hang clothing to dry, saving energy and wear and tear on the clothing.

142. Always use coupons for oil changes if you are not able to change your own oil.

143. Some companies offer tire rotation for free or a nominal charge when you purchase an oil change. This is worth the extra time and cost as it extends the life of your tires.

144. Many high schools and colleges have auto repair classes that will fix vehicles at a minimal cost.

145. Join freecycle.com; just be sure you're also willing to give stuff away.

146. Save pie tins from store bought pies or crusts to be reused.

147. Use elastic cut from clothing or fitted sheets to support plants in the garden or tie large rolls of wrapping paper.

148. If your children's school participates in the Scholastic Book Club, they offer a monthly $1.00 book deal and other low cost reading options.

149. Move credit cards over to an introductory, no interest and no transfer fees credit card and work very hard to pay it off before the 0% interest rate ends.

150. Attend free community events and concerts. Most communities have a website listing local activities or will post the events in the local newspaper. You can read the paper free at your library.

151. Make a list of every debt you owe including how much you owe to whom and make a plan to pay them off as quickly and efficiently as possible. If you don't know what you owe, it's impossible to make an effective plan.

152. Take advantage of health savings accounts (HSA) if your employer offers one.

153. If an HSA is not offered through your employer, you may be able to set up one through your local bank or credit union so long as you are enrolled in a high-deductible health plan, you are not enrolled in Medicare, you are not claimed as a dependent on someone else's taxes, and you have no other insurance. Check with your financial institution for details.

154. Check to see if there is a local recycling center or drop off location where you can drop your recyclables when out running errands; you can save a noticeable amount if you can eliminate curbside recycling service.

155. Conduct research on local financial institutions to find one that offers the lowest fees, best deposit rates, and greatest overall benefits for your needs.

156. Start putting away money for Christmas in January. Make an educated guess of what you will be spending on gifts, extra food, entertainment and travel, and then divide by 11 to figure out how much should be saved each month so you will have it to spend in December. Even if you don't start saving in January, it is never too late to start putting money away.

157. Take the time to shop around for lower cost car and home insurance.

158. Gather all your unused electronic devices and sell them. There are many places where you can sell these including eBay, decluttr, Gazelle, Amazon, FaceBook and Craigslist. Be cautious if meeting someone for a sale; make sure to meet at a well-lit, public place such as a parking lot or a police station.

159. Keep cooler bags in your vehicle so you can safely transport frozen and refrigerated foods. Don't take the chance of your food spoiling on the way home, especially in the summer. This will also allow you to take an unplanned stop if needed without worrying about your groceries.

160. If you must have juice, buy frozen concentrate; you can stretch your dollar by adding a bit more water than listed in the directions.

161. Purchase school supplies for the entire year when they go on sale several weeks before school starts. Back-to-school sales are also a great time to stock up on home office supplies.

162. If you still have a land line phone, reevaluate your needs to make sure this is still necessary.

163. If you haven't already done so, ditch cable. If broadcast television will not come in, even with an antenna, and TV is your

primary source of entertainment, go to the lowest cost package available or research to see if Netflix, Hulu, or Amazon Prime will meet your entertainment needs.

164. Save the tops of celery and carrots as they can be frozen for future use to add flavor when making broth.

165. If you find fresh berries at a good price, wash them, pat dry them dry, and place on baking sheet covered with waxed paper and freeze them individually before putting them in a freezer bag.

166. Tea bags can usually be reused up to three times. If you don't plan on using the tea bag within the next couple of hours, put it in a plastic bag with just enough water to keep it completely wet then store it in your refrigerator.

167. Cut a toilet paper or paper towel roll down one side and place it around a roll of wrapping paper to keep the paper from unraveling or around a wrapped electrical cord to keep it contained.

168. Home Depot offers free monthly workshop classes for children, as well as classes geared toward women. Visit homedepot.com/workshops for additional information.

169. Look for discounted gift cards that can be used places you normally shop or eat. You can find great savings at places like Costco, Sam's Club, raise.com, cardpool.com and others.

170. No need to buy a lint roller, just wrap tape around your hand, sticky side out, and rub over your clothing. This works just as well as a store-bought lint roller.

171. A dollar store is a great place to find inexpensive wrapping paper, gift bags, ribbon, bows and balloons for special occasions.

172. Choose and participate in hobbies that are free or have a minimal cost such as walking, biking, running, gardening, knitting, canning, cooking and reading. Physical activities will keep you healthier and new skills learned in food preparation will save you money.

173. Don't purchase more perishable foods than you can consume in a week.

174. Keep meals simple. Ingredients you don't often use could go bad before your next opportunity to cook with them.

175. Put a heating pad under the blankets 5 minutes before you go to bed to warm up the sheets. This will allow you to feel warmer and keep the house a bit cooler at night. Don't forget to turn off the heating pad before you fall asleep.

176. Turn off the stove burner just before the food in the pot is done cooking, keeping the lid on the pot; it will continue to cook and save energy. Be sure your foods are cooked to a safe temperature.

177. Turn off your oven just before the food is done baking. Keeping the oven door shut will allow the food to continue to bake yet save energy. As before, be sure you cook all foods to a safe temperature.

178. You can reuse plastic bags that didn't store meat, cheese, eggs, or anything greasy. Just wash them out and dry them on a rack.

179. Wash and reuse aluminum foil unless it covered meat or cheese.

180. Wash all plastic utensils to reuse at a later date.

181. Save all extra condiment packets from take out; these are perfect for packing in lunches or picnics or when you just need some taco sauce.

182. Grow any edibles you can at home, even if it is just a pot of herbs.

183. Before deciding to bring a pet into your home, make sure you have done the research and know how much it will cost for food, leash, collar, training, vaccinations, license, tags, medical treatment, crates and carriers.

184. Wash and cut up vegetables such carrots, celery, cucumbers, and bell peppers as soon as you get them home. Put your cut veggies in a plastic bag with a paper towel to absorb extra moisture. Storing them in bags ready to eat makes them more likely to be eaten before they can go to waste.

185. Wash fruits like grapes and strawberries and put them in a plastic bag with a paper towel to absorb moisture so they are ready to eat for a portable healthy snack. Put some in the freezer for an extra special treat.

186. Make your own basic household cleaners.

All-purpose cleaner:

- 1/2 cup of white vinegar
- 2 Tablespoons of baking soda
- 1/8 cup of water
- 10 drops of tea tree oil
- 5 drops of lemon oil

Mix vinegar, water and essential oils in a clean spray bottle, add baking soda.

Shake bottle before spraying.

Glass & mirror cleaner:

- 1/4 cup of white vinegar
- 1/4 cup isopropyl alcohol
- 2 cups of water
- 10 drops of essential oil of your choice for a better aromatic experience; lavender is a personal favorite

Toilet bowl cleaner:

Spray the inside of bowl with multi-purpose cleaner.

Sprinkle 1/2 cup baking soda and 1 package of lemon drink mix in the bowl.

Let it sit for as long as possible before scrubbing with brush.

Clean the rest of the toilet with the multi-purpose cleaner.

187. Love to read but don't have time? Check out the following FREE audiobook sites:

- Free Classic AudioBooks
- Learnoutloud
- LibriVox
- Lit2Go
- Loyal Books
- Open Culture
- Storynory

188. Drink warm beverages in the winter and cool beverages in the summer to help keep your body temperature regulated; this will allow you to adjust your thermostat with the seasons for savings.

189. Wear socks and a sweatshirt inside the house in the cooler months to feel warmer when you turn down your thermostat for savings.

190. Plug appropriate electrical devices (especially those with adapters) into power strips so when they are not in use you can

shut them all off easily to save electricity.

191. When you need a new water heater, consider a tankless unit. While they generally cost more up front, they can often yield notable energy savings by eliminating standby heat loss.

192. Keep proper air pressure in your tires for optimum gas mileage.

193. Keep a plastic bucket in the shower to collect water while you are waiting for it to heat up. This water can be used for watering plants, washing a dog, or even soaking dirty dishes. Do not use this to water plants if you have a water softener as the salt will likely kill your plants.

194. Pay with cash; people tend to spend less with cash than when paying with a check, debit or credit card.

195. When charitable solicitations arrive with useful items such as stamps, cards, coins or samples, keep them and use them without guilt or feeling pressure to make a donation. If you can't use them, pass them on or recycle them.

196. Get a job (or a second job) around the holidays; consider

stores where a discount could save you even more on your holiday plans.

197. Plastic spoons, straws, rolling pins, cookie cutters, canning lids, and popsicle sticks make great playdough toys, though they should be used under adult supervision.

198. Make your own hot cocoa mix and store in an airtight container.

- 2 cups powdered sugar
- 1 cup cocoa
- 1/2 teaspoon salt

Combine ingredients in your container.

Shake before each use to ensure an even mixture.

Warm up any type of milk you choose.

Add mixture to your taste, stir until blended and enjoy!

199. Keep individual saving accounts (sinking funds) in order to save and eventually pay for larger purchases such as a vehicle, new roof, college, or the holidays.

200. Don't throw away leftover oatmeal, make breakfast

cookies instead.

- 2 cups oatmeal
- 3 peeled and mashed ripe bananas
- 1/2 cup chopped nuts
- 1/2 cup applesauce
- 1/2 cup dried fruit
- 1 tablespoon vanilla
- 2 teaspoons cinnamon
- 3 tablespoons of your favorite sweetener

Mix ingredients thoroughly in a bowl.

Place heaping tablespoons of batter onto greased cookie sheet and gently flatten the cookie.

Bake at 350 degrees for approximately 15 minutes.

201. If you need to book a flight, be sure to check the prices with your browser in private mode. Many sites raise their prices if they can tell you've visited several times.

202. Cardboard oatmeal containers and coffee cans are great for kids to store crayons, pencils, pens, or other small trinkets. They can be decorated easily with wrapping or contact paper. Watch for sharp edges if using a metal can.

203. Save rubber bands that are used to bind your mail; they always seem to come in handy.

204. Once you're done with a notebook, cut off the covers and use the cardboard for shipping things you don't want to get bent.

205. Before you take your coins into your bank or credit union for deposit, search through them for coins of higher value. U.S. coins minted before 1965 (not pennies or nickels) are 90% silver by weight and worth far more than face value. Older coins of other origins (Canada and the U.K. just to name a couple) also have silver content. If you really want to take some time, you can also search for coins of collectible value.

206. Many employers pay or assist in paying for their employees' college tuition. These employers include Anthem, Apple, AT&T, Bank of America, Baxter, Best Buy, Boeing, BP, Chipotle, Comcast, Dunkin', FedEx, Fidelity, Home Depot, JM Smucker, Lowe's, McDonalds, Microsoft, Oracle, Procter & Gamble, Publix, Starbucks, Taco Bell, T-Mobile, UnitedHealth Group, UPS, Verizon, Walt Disney and Wells Fargo.

207. For cheap fun on a hot summer day, fill the biggest plastic storage tubs you have with water and let the kids play (with close adult supervision, of course).

208. Don't go to the mall, or do any other kind of shopping, when you are bored.

209. Write down all the reasons you are being frugal and post them in visible locations. Constant reminders of why you are saying no to purchases, or working extra hours makes your journey a bit easier.

210. If you are able, consider selling plasma; some places give you bonuses after giving a certain number of times.

211. Prepare meals at home. This is cheaper and often much healthier than eating out.

212. Purchase staples – such as beans, oats, popcorn and other grains – in bulk.

213. Health departments offer low or no costs vaccinations.

214. Last year's calendar can be turned into cheap artwork. Repurpose old frames or find them at a dollar or thrift store or garage sale where they are cheap. Calendars usually have a

theme; the framed pictures will look nice grouped together.

215. Make a budget plan to pay off all credit cards as quickly as possible. While opinions vary on how best to approach this task, mathematically speaking, you will usually save the most money by eliminating the highest rate cards first.

216. Do not use store credit cards as they tend to have the highest interests rates.

217. Do not purchase items "__ months same as cash" unless you already have the money in the bank to pay. Many people are not able to pay off the full amount in the required time and then have to pay all the interest accumulated since time of purchase.

218. If you use pine kitty litter, you can purchase pine horse pellets. They are very similar in size, work just as well, and cost less.

219. If you need dental work, use a local dental college for cheaper options.

220. For a low cost haircut, find a local cosmetology school and make an appointment. If you keep your hair very short, consider

buying your own clippers; once you've cut your own hair a couple of times – and have avoided that many trips to the barber – they will have paid for themselves.

221. Need a quiet retreat? Some convents and monasteries offer rooms to rent; this is often much cheaper and more memorable than a hotel.

222. If you have AAA, make sure you are aware of all of the discounts offered on hotels, rental cars, restaurants, and some shopping.

223. Check out all of the free entertainment in your area. Most cities, even small ones, have a website that lists local events and activities.

224. In addition to religious services, many houses of worship offer free events including concerts, exercise classes, plays and playgroups.

225. Use freeclinics.com to find free or low-cost medical care.

226. Watch frugal, money saving, and budgeting videos on YouTube to give you additional ideas and keep you motivated.

227. Check out websites like thefrugalsource.com to find resources for saving money and more.

228. Can't afford babysitting? Join or start a babysitting co-op to keep it free.

229. No decorations for your Christmas tree? Pine cones and holly clippings make a beautiful addition. Paper chains can be made with what you have on hand and stringing popcorn can make the tree look more festive. Once the holiday is over, put the string outside for the birds.

230. Make homemade decorations (this is a recipe you'll likely want to tweak to your preference):

- 3/4 cup of applesauce
- 1 cup of cinnamon
- 4 tablespoons of liquid white glue

Mix ingredients thoroughly and roll out the dough between layers of waxed paper (or cereal bags). The thinner the dough the faster it will dry, but the harder it will be to handle. Cut out shapes and punch a hole at the top so when they dry you can put a string through in order to hang them from the tree. They look like cookies and smell amazing, so make sure your kids don't eat them.

231. Another sweet smelling ornament can be made by tying a decorative ribbon around a lime, lemon or clementine so it can be hung from tree or in your closet. Insert whole cloves into the skin of the fruit making sure to leave some space to account for shrinkage.

232. Stock up on items when they are deeply discounted. Here is a general guideline on grocery items that are discounted each month.

January - vitamins, diet foods, snack foods, frozen diet meals, oatmeal

February - frozen waffles, oatmeal, oriental food ingredients, chocolate

March - frozen foods

April - ham, eggs, baking supplies

May - salsa, chips, paper plates, plastic utensils, chips, hamburger, hot dogs, buns and condiments

June - dairy items

July - hot dogs, hamburgers, buns, chips, dips and condiments

August - individual snacks, lunchmeat, lunchables, cold cereal, frozen breakfast foods

September - diabetic foods, bread, tomato products

October - pumpkin, candy, apple products, baking supplies

November - turkey, dressing, pumpkin, baking supplies, coffee and tea

December - bread, rolls, baking supplies, ham, egg nog, pie filling, snacks, soda and champagne

233. Go meatless at least once a week, giving your grocery budget a break.

234. Use meat as a condiment, instead as a main ingredient. Ingredients such as beans, lentils and oatmeal can stretch meat in recipes.

235. Go to wowbrary.org to see if your library participates in this program. If so, you can sign up to receive a weekly email listing all new materials your library has ordered, allowing you to request holds on the things you want.

236. Plant perennial herbs including thyme, chives, sage, French tarragon, and mint (mint can be invasive).

237. Use small cardboard boxes to give your cat places to hide or nap.

238. Watch movies and TV shows for free on VUDU.

239. If you have an addiction, please get help, not only to improve your mental and physical health but your family life and finances as well.

- Substance Abuse and Mental Health Services Administration 1-800-662-HELP (4357)
- National Suicide Prevention Hotline 1-800-273-TALK (8255)
- 1-800-QUIT-NOW (1-800-784-8669) to help you reach a smoke free life
- National Problem Gambling Hotline 1-800-522-4700

240. Make your own beef jerky

- 2-3 pounds of eye of round, London broil or similar lean cut of meat cut into thin slices - it helps if the meat is slightly frozen
- 2/3 cup of Worcestershire sauce
- 2/3 soy sauce, or coconut aminos

Everything else is a matter of your personal flavor choices but may include:

- garlic powder
- sugar

- onion powder
- liquid smoke
- honey
- smoked paprika
- red pepper flakes
- hot sauce

Mix your chosen ingredients in a bowl. Place the meat in the bowl, cover, and place in the refrigerator for at least an hour (vary time to your taste). Place in dehydrator on appropriate setting until done (a minimum of 4 hours). It should break if bent. Store in air tight container.

241. Invest in a simple dehydrator. This will allow you to make beef jerky and do so much more, like dehydrating your surplus of herbs, fruits, and veggies. The dried fruit can be added to your homemade granola.

242. Need to rent some equipment for a DIY project? Check with your neighbors, friends and/or family to see if they could use the equipment too, then split the cost of rental.

243. Heading to the drive- in? Spend some extra time prepping before you go. Pop your own popcorn, make your own food, and bring your own drinks. One of our local drive-in theaters shows

3 movies on Friday and Saturday evenings, so we make a complete dinner to eat. It's a lot of work but it saves money and makes extra special memories.

244. Make sure your home is properly insulated.

245. Check to make sure all the gaps around your home are sealed.

246. Most electrical companies will do a free home energy audit. Check to see if yours does and if so, schedule an appointment.

247. Going on a road trip? Pack your own food and drinks; it's cheaper and healthier.

248. If you don't have a cooler, you can keep food warm or cool by wrapping it tightly in a paper bag or newspaper, then wrap blankets around the wrapped food. It should keep cool/hot for several hours.

249. Pack ice cubes in quart or gallon zipper bags to place in your cooler. This keeps the food from getting wet and ruined from the melting ice.

250. If you're ordering something from Amazon that you don't need immediately, choose a slower shipping option at checkout and get a financial credit towards Prime Pantry or, occasionally, digital media.

251. Use one of the following free budget apps to keep track of your money:

- everydollar.com
- mint.com
- goodbudget.com
- nerdwallet.com
- honeyfi.com
- dollarbird.co
- wally.me
- claritymoney.com
- fudget.com
- spendee.com

252. Review every single bill that you receive to make sure it is accurate. Billing mistakes happen and you shouldn't have to pay for them.

253. Renting a car? Check to see if your car insurance covers you so you don't purchase rental car insurance unnecessarily.

254. After Christmas, purchase red items for Valentine's Day and green for St. Patrick's Day such as plates, napkins and cookie decorations.

255. If you are lucky enough that friends and family are asking what you'd want for a gift, be sure to ask for gift cards to places you already frequent such as your favorite grocery store, gas station, or a drug store. You can save the gift cards for when money is extra tight or you can use the money you would have otherwise spent on those items to increase savings or to speed payoff of any debt you might still have.

256. Spend a few minutes each week to make a meal plan. Knowing what you are going to have for each meal of the week (plus snacks) allows you to purchase only groceries that you need, so nothing goes to waste.

257. Post the meal plan on the fridge so everyone knows what will be served for each meal and prevent the ingredients intended for those meals from being used before they are needed.

258. Extra milk that is about to go bad? Pour some out of the jug and place in freezer for later.

259. If you buy deeply discounted shredded cheese, you can freeze some for later use in recipes that require baking. Place packaged cheese inside a freezer bag before placing in freezer.

260. Find the lowest gas prices in your area on gasbuddy.com

261. Lower the temperature of your water heater to 120 degrees Fahrenheit, unless you have a suppressed immune system, then it should be kept at 140 degrees Fahrenheit. The higher temperature will increase the chance of scalding so be careful.

262. Many places offer some free or low cost medicines with no membership required including: Amigos United Supermarkets, Bi Lo, Giant Eagle, Kroger, Market Street Pharmacies, Meijer, Price Chopper, Publix Supermarket, Reasor's Foods, Schnuck's Pharmacies, ShopRite Stores, WalMart and Wegmans.

263. Always ask your healthcare provider to prescribe generic medicines whenever possible.

264. If you go to pick up a prescription and the cost is too much,

you can always ask the pharmacist to call your health care professional and see if there is another option available.

265. Create a master list of special events that take place each month. Be sure to include any holidays you celebrate, birthdays, anniversaries, and family reunions so you can plan accordingly when you budget each month.

266. Whenever your healthcare provider prescribes medication or supplements, be sure to ask if they have samples available so you can try it before you buy it.

267. Shred all personal papers before throwing them out to reduce your chances of identity theft.

268. Use grocery apps that pay you back for doing what you already do, shop for groceries. There are now too many grocery apps to list but here are a few: Checkout 51, Coupon Sherpa, Coupons.com, Favado, Food on the Table, Grocery IQ, Ibotta, Receipt Hog, SavingStar and Shopkick.

269. Paying insurance on a monthly basis tends to cost more. Save your money so you are able to pay the bill in full yearly and save the upcharge for having a monthly billing statement.

270. Pay off credit card balances in full each month; otherwise you are giving your money away.

271. Purchase your vehicles used and drive them "until the wheels fall off". It's generally cheaper to make repairs than to purchase a new vehicle and pay interest over 5-7 years. A new vehicle can lose 20% of its value as soon as you drive it off the lot.

272. Enjoy free music with Grooveshark, MOG FreePay, Pandora, Spotify and YouTube.

273. You can wash windows and mirrors with newspapers, instead of paper towels, for a streak free clean.

274. It's free to join Angie's List to check ratings of service providers; be sure to check for deals and coupons.

275. Get rid of storage units. Add up the yearly cost and see if what you are storing is actually worth it. If you don't use the items in storage regularly you probably do not need the stuff. Sell it and use the money to pay off debt. You'll also save the money you had been spending for the storage unit.

276. Combine coupons with sales for items you purchase regularly.

277. Most vehicles can go more than 3,000 miles before changing the oil. Check the owner's manual to be sure you know the recommended intervals for your vehicle.

278. When purchasing new appliances, always check a scratch and dent store first. Really, who cares if the side of a dryer has a scratch, the kids will more than likely add to it!

279. Find a Habitat for Humanity store in your area (https://www.habitat.org/restores) for building materials, appliances, and furniture. You'll save money and help the local Habitat in their mission.

280. Always shop the clearance section of your grocery store first, but be sure to only purchase what you need.

281. Write "Ask for ID" on the back of your credit card instead of your signature. You really don't want someone to have your signature and your credit card if you lose it.

282. Limit screen time for kids; the more advertising they see,

the more they want you to buy.

283. If using disposable plastic cups and utensils for a party, save them. Most can easily be washed and dried by hand. If you're too embarrassed to tell your guests that you plan to reuse the plasticware, just put out a box or bag labeled "recycling" and ask that they be placed there instead of the trash.

284. If you drink, drink at home. There is a huge mark up on alcohol at bars and restaurants that can range from 200 - 500%. Also, misjudging your ability to drive just once can cost a ton of money and so much more.

285. Don't buy single-serve bottles while out and about. Single bottles can cost just pennies less (and sometimes actually cost more) than a 2 liter bottle on sale.

286. Check out your local ethnic grocery stores. They can be cheaper for produce and ingredients that are less popular at big box stores.

287. Remember to breathe. Yes, I know you are breathing right now, but we tend to take shallow breaths. Deeper breaths result in a state of calm and clearer thinking allowing you to be more productive during the day.

288. Make your own hummus.

- 2 cups cooked chickpeas
- 1/2 cup tahini
- 1/4 cup extra virgin olive oil
- Juice of one lemon
- Garlic powder to taste
- Onion powder to taste
- Sea salt to taste
- Pepper to taste

Put all ingredients into a food processor and blend until smooth; store in an airtight container in the refrigerator.

289. Always shop for textbooks online before purchasing at a college bookstore.

290. Barter for goods and services. While it is a different way of thinking and requires a bit more time and effort, it can be very rewarding for those who participate. Effective barter could be as simple as watching each other's pets, swapping eggs for haircuts, or picking up kids from school in exchange for baked bread. Search for barter groups in your local area to find like-minded individuals. Places to start are: babysitterexchange.com,

craigslist.org, gametz.com, paperbackswap.com, swapacd.com, swapadvd.com and u-exchange.com.

291. Never go to the grocery store hungry. Eat something before you go, hunger can break your grocery budget.

292. Reuse birthday decorations. Birthday signs, streamers and balloon weights can all be saved and used for another celebration. Purchase decorations in neutral colors so they can be used for anyone of any age. To make it extra special, write the person and date that the sign was used for each time it is used; a little history in the making.

293. Never pay full price for a book. Discount books can be found everywhere: garage sales, thrift stores, discount bookstores, discount tables at regular bookstores, and sales through Barnes & Noble and Amazon.

294. If you find yourself stressed, try meditating a few minutes each day. By reducing stress, you will be better focused and more productive during your day.

295. Try a spending fast. This is a very popular way to decrease your spending. Pick two months a year to severely restrict spending, only purchasing what is absolutely necessary.

It can be just as helpful to pick a week out of each month to only spend money on that which is absolutely necessary. Make sure not to overspend when the fast is completed.

296. Don't throw away canned goods just because they have passed their best by date. Most canned goods have an expiration date 1-4 years after purchase, but if the cans are kept in a cool, dark place and in good condition without dents, they can last from 3-6 years and probably much longer.

In a few rare cases, canned foods have been proven to be still safe more than 100 years after being canned. Check out the story of the steamboat Bertrand for more details.

297. Accept hand-me-downs and used items from other people gratefully. Once people know that you are willing to accept used items, you will start to receive more than you can use. Graciously thank them and pass along what you are not able to use.

298. Starbucks bags their used coffee grounds and give them free to anyone who asks. These are great for your garden and landscaping, especially for acid-loving plants like evergreens.

299. After Thanksgiving, Easter, or any other big meal celebrations, use the leftovers to make yourself complete dinners on sturdy disposable plates (think TV dinner).

300. Unpaired socks are perfect for dusting the house.

301. Make it a point to return items that are defective, spoiled, wrong size, etc., otherwise you are literally throwing money away. Keep the returnable items in their bags with the receipts and place near your keys so you have a reminder each time you leave the house.

302. Review your credit card statement monthly for charges you didn't make. Also, be sure to cancel any subscriptions you no longer want.

303. Need something pressed and aren't able to iron? Throw it in the dryer for a few minutes, just make sure to take it out immediately and hang it up.

304. No matter where you are spending your money – whether it's a hotel, hospital, store, or a repair shop – always ask for an itemized bill and review it for accuracy.

305. Insulate outdoor spigots in the colder months to keep them from freezing and possibly bursting.

306. When it is very cold outside, open the cabinet doors under faucets against outside walls and keep the water faucet trickling to keep the pipes from freezing.

307. There are numerous sites that offer free classes. The following is just a small sample:

- AcademicEarth.org,
- Codeacademy.com
- Coursera.org
- Futurelearn.com
- KhanAcademy.org
- OpenCulture.com
- Open2study.com
- TheGymnasium.com

308. Set up a Microsoft account and search the web with Bing to earn points toward gift cards.

309. Roll up a bath towel and put it at the base of exterior doors to keep out drafts.

310. If you have a hard time staying within your grocery budget,

try ordering your groceries online and picking them up at the store with curbside pick-up. Many stores offer this service including Walmart, Kroger, Meijer, and Target.

311. Send away for any rebates immediately so you don't forget. Also, make copies of the relevant receipts and any other documentation in case you do not receive your rebate.

312. If you want to give back but cannot afford to give financially to charity, volunteering is a wonderful way to help others in need and to experience contentment with what you already have. Don't forget to keep track of your mileage as it may be tax deductible.

313. Do not purchase dry-clean only clothing if it is something you will wear frequently.

314. Make your own baby food. It's easy to do, costs much less than store-bought baby food, and it's preservative free. Freeze your homemade baby food in ice cube trays and store it in freezer bags (with like kinds) for later use.

315. When purchasing produce look to see whether it is sold by the item or by weight. Cucumbers, peppers, and other veggies are usually sold by the piece so you want to go big!

316. Cut the bottom off of milk jugs to cover seedlings if the weather makes a turn for the worse. This will protect any investment you have in the seedlings and – if your thumb is green enough – save you money down the road when you get produce from your garden instead of the store.

317. If you can't afford curtains, you can tape newspaper to the windows using blue painter's tape. It's easy to take off and the tape can be reused multiple times.

318. Bathe small children together to save on water and time.

319. If you have an unexpected breakout, you can reduce it with aspirin. Simply crush an aspirin and add enough water to make a thick paste. Place the paste on the pimple and let dry completely before washing it off. The salicylic acid in aspirin works as an anti-inflammatory to help reduce the size and redness.

320. If you don't have time to wash your hair, just sprinkle arrowroot flour, cornstarch, or baking powder at the roots and brush it through your hair.

321. If you're traveling and need to stay in a hotel, look for a place with a refrigerator and microwave so you can bring your own food and reduce the cost of your trip.

322. Also, when staying in a hotel, look for one with a free breakfast.

323. Some hotels, like the Drury Inn, offer not only free breakfast but also a free dinner and drinks with popcorn and soda in the evenings.

324. Get life insurance when you are young and healthy making it much cheaper than waiting.

325. When traveling, use the shampoo, conditioner and soap provided by the hotel. This not only saves money, but reduces what you need to pack. Also, be sure to extend your savings by taking home any used bars or bottles you didn't finish as they'd otherwise just go into the trash.

326. If you eat cereal most mornings, switch to oatmeal once or twice a week to save money.

327. When planning time out with friends, find a place that offers free refills on drinks.

328. As your kids get older, have them start paying their own bills. This does not need to be an all or none event. Instead, have them take on part of their phone bill, or car insurance and add to it as time goes on. Not only are you saving money right now, this can pay additional dividends down the road as you are teaching your children to be more self-reliant and less likely to depend on you for future financial needs.

329. If you do need to continue to live with your parents or move back in with them, make it a mutually beneficial arrangement. You can help out with monthly expenses and do designated chores around the house, making it cheaper than living on your own and helping your parent(s) out at the same time.

330. When having work done at your home, check to see if the service provider offers a cash discount. Make sure you get a receipt.

331. Having a ham dinner? Save the ham bone and use it to flavor beans. You can always freeze the bone until needed.

332. Use old Mylar balloons as gift bags or wrapping paper

333. Roast the seeds from your Halloween pumpkins for a tasty snack.

Soak pumpkin seeds in filtered water overnight with sea salt to taste.

Drain the water, and then mix in enough oil to lightly coat the seeds. Add a bit more salt and bake on the lowest temperature on middle oven rack.

Turn every 15 minutes until seeds are dry and crispy. Once cool, store the seeds in an air tight container.

334. Left over decorating pumpkins, especially pie pumpkins, can be cooked and used for baking. Cut pumpkins in half and place open side down into a baking pan. Fill pan with an inch or more of water and bake at 350 degrees Fahrenheit until a butter knife goes through the pumpkin easily. Let cool. Scoop into containers, put in refrigerator overnight. On the following day drain out all the water you can. The pumpkin is now ready to use for baking or to freeze for future use.

335. Track the prices of things you buy regularly – whether in a notebook, spreadsheet, or other app – so that you'll know when you see a really good price. Over time, you may be able to identify patterns in pricing which would allow you to anticipate and budget for stocking up.

336. Carry coupons with you at all times. This will ensure that you are ready to save – and avoid frustration – when saving opportunities arise.

337. Save heavy duty bags to throw away broken items. We save chicken feed bags and bulk grain bags to put broken glass in before putting it in the regular trash bag. This will keep the trash bag from being cut and wasted, and will protect you and the trash hauler from injury. If you don't have heavy duty bags to save, you can use a cardboard box or paper grocery sack (be sure to tape it shut) to contain the pieces.

338. Learn how to cook. There are numerous beginners' cookbooks to be found at the library and an almost infinite number of recipes on the internet. This will save you lots of money and can keep you healthier.

339. If you're out to eat and you still have some of your drink left in your glass, don't be embarrassed to request a take-out cup. Not all places will do this, but I have found that most will as you have paid for that drink. Obviously, this is for non-alcoholic beverages only.

340. If you are at a fast food restaurant that offers free self-serve refills on drinks, always top off your drink before you leave. Even if you don't want more today, you can always put it in the fridge for later. This works especially well with tea.

341. Start stocking up on cold and flu supplies in early fall while

they are on sale. Not only will you save money but you'll avoid having to go out when you're actually sick and you'd rather just rest.

342. When you move, make sure get any utility deposits returned.

343. During the summer, cook outside on the grill or fire pit to avoid heating up the house.

344. Only run your dishwasher when it is completely full.

345. Thanksgiving season is the time to stock up on turkeys for the year. Many stores offer free or deeply-discounted turkeys once you've spent a certain amount.

346. Many financial institutions and insurance agencies will send out free life insurance offers through the mail, usually around $1,000. Take advantage of this; fill out the paperwork, and be sure to make a copy to put into your files.

347. To keep your grocery budget under control before big holiday meals, plan your menu at least a month ahead of time and start shopping sales, buying extra items a little at a time.

348. Start a gift closet, bin, or shelf. When you're out and find items that are deeply discounted and would be appreciated by people you know, buy them and put them away. When birthdays, holidays, or other special occasions roll around, you'll have gifts ready to go.

349. Make sure free is actually free. A free pet will end up costing you hundreds, if not thousands of dollars in food, vet bills, and accessories. Free shipping isn't free if you have to spend more than you intended to qualify. Also, when going to a store or other venue to get something free, be sure to weigh the cost of gas and the value of your time against that of the "free" item.

350. Check out free birthday treats or meals offered by many restaurants and stores. There are just too many to list here, but you can do a web search and view the numerous offers.

351. Make sure that you review all of your employee benefits every year from health insurance to HSA accounts to commuter benefits. Circumstances change and your elections should reflect such changes.

352. Only purchase a home that you can afford to buy with a 15 year mortgage. You'll save a small fortune on interest.

353. If you use outside lights to decorate for holidays, put them on a timer or a photosensor to avoid wasting electricity during the day.

354. Have a low-maintenance hair style.

355. Only print what is absolutely necessary. Printers are often sold below cost; the real money is made through the consumables (ink and toner).

356. In my experience, off-brand toner has worked just as well as the name brand.

357. Many Christmas tree lots will give you cut off boughs for free, especially closer to Christmas. You can use them to make wreaths or other decorations for holiday savings.

358. Purchasing k-cups at full price is still cheaper than purchasing coffee out.

359. If you have a small area to paint, go to a hardware or paint store and look for discounted cans of paint. You can save a lot of money if you're flexible with your color.

360. Flip and rotate your mattress regularly to extend its life.

361. If you enjoy reading daily devotions, many can be found for free online instead of purchasing them in book form.

362. When shopping for an engagement ring, there is no rule that says it must be a diamond. Consider other stones that may have more meaning, like birthstones, or gems with significant color or a unique shape.

363. If you're looking for a meaningful and low cost birthday gift, choose to spend the day with the birthday girl/boy giving them your undivided attention for the entire day. Go to a park, have a picnic, get dessert at their favorite restaurant, cook their favorite meal at home, or simply pick an amount of money to be spent and let them choose what to do with it on their day.

364. For pizza and movie night, have everyone make their own individual pizza at home and check out a movie from the library or search your own collection and watch an old favorite. If you can't decide on a movie, consider having a game night.

365. Pay extra on your mortgage every month, no matter how

small the amount; make sure it goes towards principal (note: most, but not all mortgages allow this). This will lower the amount of interest paid over the life of the loan resulting in you paying less on the house in the long run.

366. Cook more recipes with cheaper but still healthful ingredients such as russet potatoes, onions, cabbage, sweet potatoes, eggs, rice, beans, lentils, and canned tomatoes.

367. Wash outside windows in the fall so more light and warmth will stream in during the winter months.

368. Place a water bottle filled with water in the toilet tank so less water is used to flush the toilet.

369. If you're out of toothpaste, just use a little baking soda and water and rinse well.

370. Purchase unisex clothing, coats, jackets, shoes and boots for babies and toddlers so they can be passed down to siblings.

371. Purchase large bottles of hand soap to refill individual containers. Fill approximately 3/4 with soap and the rest with water and shake extremely well.

372. If you eat yoghurt, purchase a large container and put in small reusable plastic containers for snacks and lunches.

373. Purchase meat in bulk (e.g. whole, half or quarter animal), it is so much cheaper by the pound.

374. To keep yourself from eating out at lunchtime, prepare meals on Sunday so you will have food for the week.

375. If you enjoy background noise, opt for the radio vs. the TV as it requires less energy.

376. When planning a get together, make it a potluck so everyone can share their favorite dishes and the expense will be shared by all.

377. While in debt, stop adding to any collections you may have such as sports cards or shot glasses. Instead, use that money and time to pay down your debt.

378. Save for medical expenses every month. Even if you are not ill, eventually something will happen; an unexpected trip to

ER is expensive. Make sure to put this money in a separate account.

379. Wash delicates by hand and hang to dry; they will last longer.

380. Use bath towels more than once, especially in the winter when you are less dirty. Just hang them to dry somewhere they will receive proper ventilation.

381. Don't flush products other than toilet paper. If you do, you risk costly repairs whether you are on a septic system or public sewer.

382. When you sell surplus items, immediately use the proceeds toward retiring debt or into savings, as appropriate (debt first!).

383. Go make-up free for a day or more each week. Let your face breathe and your natural beauty shine!

384. Many utility companies will allow you to get on a monthly budget plan where you pay approximately the same amount each month, which can make budgeting easier.

385. Repurpose kitty litter buckets. There are so many ingenious ways to reuse these including, pet food storage, storage for kids toys, cat condos, strawberry planter, cat feeding station, watering can, garage storage, craft supplies, trash cans, and nesting boxes for chickens to name just a few.

386. Spend less time on social media. Social media continuously bombards us with activities, goods, and stories that make you feel as if you are missing out on something. We often begin to compare our lives to others leading to discontentment and overspending to keep up. If you still want to spend time on social media, follow others who are trying to pay off debt and living a frugal life.

387. Don't set yourself up to fail. If you know you can't resist purchasing items in a specific store, simply don't go.

388. Make sure to include a little fun money in your monthly budget. This will make it much easier to stick to your budget when you know you can have a bit of fun too.

389. Don't purchase pre-made craft kits for kids. The cheap ones are worthless and the expensive ones are too much money for what is included. Kids are more creative when given supplies and the freedom to create as they wish, with supervision.

390. Don't purchase souvenirs while on vacation. What looks cute away from home will just add clutter to your house and end up being tossed aside sooner rather than later. It's better to take pictures to record the memories or have a copy of a menu or a receipt of a fun activity to put in a scrap book.

391. When you pay cash for anything or make a payment towards your debt, always get a receipt, even if you are close to the person you are paying.

392. Keep track of monthly bills such as water, electric, and gas. This will encourage you to take steps to keep your bills lower.

393. Do not sign up for any free trials that require a credit card. Most people get busy and forget to unsubscribe and are out at least one month's subscription fee.

394. Freeze your credit while you are getting out of debt, forcing extra effort if you are tempted to sign up for another card or make a purchase on store credit.

395. Use futureme.org to send yourself an encouraging letter about what you hope to have accomplished financially in the next

one, three or five years.

396. Make a list of 12 ways you could save money that you aren't currently doing. Add one per month into your lifestyle over the next year.

397. Don't carry an ATM or credit card in your wallet on a daily basis.

398. Put your emergency fund in separate account (i.e. don't just keep the in your checking account). You want to be able to access it when needed, but not too easily.

399. If you typically get big income tax refunds, adjust your withholding. There is no reason to allow the government to keep your money all year, interest free. The IRS website has a withholding calculator to help you adjust appropriately.

400. Look into refinancing your mortgage at a lower interest rate.

401. Pay your bills on time so you can maintain or improve your credit score. A better credit score means you pay a lower interest rate if you absolutely have to use your credit.

402. Write out your financial goals for the next year, five years, ten years, and beyond. When you actually write your goals down it makes you think about where you want to be in the future and makes your goals more real. If your goals change, you can always rewrite them. This is a great opportunity – with the TV off and phones put away – to discuss your financial future with your spouse.

403. Go to libraryextension.com and you can download their Chrome extension. As you browse media on sites like Amazon or Barnes and Noble, the extension will let you know if the title is available at your local library. It's free to use and if your library isn't already included you can use the form on the site to request they add it.

404. Watch your ATM usage. Most banks and credit unions limit the number of transactions you can make per month; go over, and you'll likely pay a fee. Plan ahead and take cash out only once or twice a month so if you have an emergency you'll still have transactions left. You can also avoid fees by making sure to use only ATMs your bank owns or that are in a network to which your bank belongs.

405. Make sure that money withdrawn from your emergency fund is actually for an emergency. Vacations, a new car, and gifts are not emergencies. Don't do long-lasting harm for a

fleeting feeling.

406. Keep some powdered milk in your pantry. It has a long shelf life and it can be made quickly. This keeps you from having to run out at the last minute to purchase milk should you run out.

407. If your state has a tax free day, save for it! Go to freetaxweekend.com to see which states participate and what is included.

408. Cook large pieces of meat such as whole chickens or a roast. Use what you need for a meal or two now and freeze any extra for later.

409. Go to malwarebytes.com and download their free software to enhance your computer's security.

410. If you're boiling eggs, boil a lot. Eggs are cheap and nutritious and they're easy to add to greens or turn into egg salad for a quick meal to help you avoid the drive thru.

411. Reduce the amount of laundry you do by only washing clothes when they are truly dirty. Many pants, dresses and skirts can be worn multiple times.

412. Purchase a big package of the same type of socks so that, as they wear out, you will be able to continually match them with others.

413. Make your own reusable ice pack. Pour one cup of alcohol and two cups of water into a freezer bag. Remove as much air as possible from the bag. Put the bag into another freezer bag and place it in freezer.

414. Store NiMH batteries in the freezer to significantly extend their life; be sure let them warm to room temperature before using.

415. Purchase cheaper cuts of meat and cook on low in a slow cooker for a longer time with water or salad dressing depending on how you are going to use the meat.

416. Mix the following to make your own basic salad dressing

- 1/2 cup olive oil
- 1/4 cup vinegar (rice, balsamic, or apple cider vinegar

Optional:

- garlic

- salt
- pepper
- lemon zest or lemon squeeze

Keep in an air-tight container in the refrigerator; glass is best. Shake when ready to use.

417. Use dried beans instead of canned. Although this takes more planning, they are much cheaper.

418. Make a grocery list and stick to it; remember to bring it with you.

419. Take a moment to answer surveys on receipts. You could win money or free food.

420. Reduce what you use every day. A one tablespoon per day reduction would save over 22 cups of food a year.

421. If you need a break from working on your computer, consider playing a game beneficial to humanity instead of shopping online. At freerice.com, every question you answer correctly donates 10 grains of rice via the World Food Programme

422. If there is a huge sale on butter, stock up. Salted butter can be stored in freezer for up to a year, unsalted for up to 6 months. Just put the butter sticks in a freezer bag and remove as much air as possible before freezing.

423. Save broken flower pots to use at the bottom of other pots for drainage.

424. Is there a local attraction that your family enjoys visiting on a regular basis? It may be financially beneficial to purchase an annual pass. This would allow you to visit whenever you like and not feel compelled to stay all day to "get your money's worth".

425. Change your furnace filter regularly to allow your furnace to run more efficiently.

426. When you've finished a jar of pickles, save the juice and add sliced cucumbers. Let it set in the refrigerator at least 24 hours for more "pickles".

427. Don't feel compelled to keep up with the latest technology. The new phone, tablet, or laptop will just cost you more money

with little benefit. Keep what you have and use it until it breaks. You'll save a small fortune.

428. If leftovers are not eaten within 24 hours put them in the freezer. Soup can be eaten when you want a quick light meal; veggies can be added to soups and casseroles; meat can be used for soup, tacos or casseroles; and fruit and vegetables – even lettuce – can be used in smoothies.

429. Does the honey in your jar look like a dark solid mass? Don't throw it out. Pure honey is good indefinitely but will crystalize over time. Just place it in a warm spot in your kitchen or put the bottle in pot of very warm water and it will slowly return to its liquid form.

430. When buying meat in bulk (whole, half, or quarter) always ask the processor for everything, including bones for broth or your dog, liver, and any other parts that can be legally obtained in your state. Liver is wonderful to have mixed into your ground beef to add extra flavor and nutrients.

431. Be mindful of your actions throughout the day. Think about everything, whether it's how much toilet paper or how many paper towels you use in a day, how much and what type of food you are eating, or where and why you are driving to each store. The more you ponder these things, the more opportunities

for efficiency and savings will come to mind.

432. Purchase all store brand items, whether food or personal care items. They are often the same product as the national brands with a different label, and they usually cost less.

433. For hours of free entertainment over the internet, check out radio.garden. This site allows you to listen to radio station feeds from around the world.

434. Misplaced bills can cost you late fees or even being sent to collections. Be sure to open your mail immediately and put all bills, and other mail requiring follow up, in a designated spot to ensure they are easy to find when you need them. Also, recycle or shred what you don't need right away to minimize clutter.

435. Make sure to budget for stamps. Even if you pay all of your bills electronically, you'll want to make sure you have stamps for a birthday card or any other items that must be sent snail mail. You will avoid having to make a last minute trip to the post office wasting, both time and money.

436. Increase the time you spend doing physically and mentally healthy activities, games, exercise, yoga, meditation, hobbies, and learning; this will increase your well-being and bring more

contentment.

437. Spend some time cleaning out your inbox. Unsubscribe from all the sources enticing you to purchase things promising to make you happy, skinny, popular or healthy.

438. Unsubscribe from catalogues. This does take some time as you may have to call each business and ask to be removed from their mailing list. But, if you might be tempted to make impulse purchases, it's worth the effort to prevent them from coming into your home.

439. Whenever you can, avoid storing your credit card when making internet purchases. While minimizing the number of places the card is stored does reduce the risk of it being included in a data breach, the big benefit from forcing yourself to enter the card information each time is that you will have to spend more time thinking about and making the purchase; it's one last opportunity to ask yourself whether you actually need the thing you're about to buy.

440. Install LED lights as bulbs go out; while initially more expensive than other options, you'll save money in the long run as they use less energy than even CFLs and can last much longer.

441. Save and reuse gift bags.

442. Be careful shopping at warehouse stores. Since you have to buy in bulk, food can spoil before it is eaten, so have a plan for how you will use it.

443. Get your financial paperwork in order. There is nothing more annoying than being unable to find necessary documentation at tax time. Plus, having everything on hand when you start will minimize overall time and frustration, and will prevent errors of omission and the need to file revisions.

444. Add vinegar to your dishwasher to make the dishes less spotty. This is cheaper than anti-spotting agents and reduces your exposure to chemicals.

445. Set appropriate limits for money to be spent on gifts for all occasions and stick to those limits.

446. When appropriate, skip gifts all together and enjoy a low-cost experience. Memories from experiences last a lifetime; most gifts don't.

447. Check your vehicle's air filter. Replacing a dirty air filter

can increase your MPG on a vehicle up to 10%.

448. You need to establish an emergency fund. Emergencies will happen; it's just a matter of time.

449. Repair clothing immediately before the tear becomes too big to fix.

450. If you have to choose between saving for retirement and paying for college for your kids, you must make a selfish decision. Retirement will be here before you know it and your children can work and save for college.

451. If you are curious about how much you will be receiving from social security, go to www.ssa.org/myaccount. This will give you motivation to start saving more money.

452. You may have money you don't even know about. Go to unclaimed.org to see if you have money waiting for you. Each state has its own website; be sure to check in all the states you've ever lived.

453. Shop for clothing at thrift stores; better yet, shop at thrift stores on discount days.

454. Paying your mortgage bi-weekly results in the equivalent of 13 full payments per year and knocks approximately 8 years off a 30-year fixed rate mortgage. Check with your lender to see how you can do this.

455. Take advantage of your financial institution's savings vehicles. Some offer Christmas accounts, HSAs, and savings challenges.

456. Check out discount thrift stores such as Goodwill Outlet where you pay by the pound.

457. Save all buttons that come off new clothing in a button jar, just like your grandmother use to do. You just never know when a button will save your favorite shirt!

458. If you have a lot of medical appointments keep track of them on your calendar. Be sure to record your round trip mileage and other costs such as parking expenses or bus fare as they may be tax deductible.

459. If you live in a state with bottle returns, keep your bottles somewhere that is enough out of the way that you won't get

frustrated and toss them, yet convenient enough to remember to put them in the car when heading to the store.

460. Don't purchase a home with a monthly mortgage payment more than 25% of your monthly take-home pay.

461. If you need a rug to cover a hard surface floor, consider a carpet remnant instead. They are generally much cheaper than rugs of the same size. You will want to be sure to have the edges bound to prevent fraying and rolling. You can do this yourself, but many stores that sell remnants will do the binding for a nominal fee.

462. Pull your credit report at least once a year. You can get one report from each credit bureau (TransUnion, Experian, and Exquifax) per year. Take advantage of these free reports to make sure you have no fraudulent activity or incorrect information.

463. Do not increase your lifestyle when you get a raise. Use that extra money to pay off debt, save for retirement, or save toward a goal in one of your sinking funds.

464. If you own a good pair of shoes that you like and fit well, paying for a repair instead of a new pair may be the way to go.

465. If your leather shoes are getting a little too snug, you don't need to buy shoe stretchers. Just put on a thick pair of socks, put on the leather or suede shoes and heat the snug spots with a hair dryer on high heat. Wiggle your toes and move your feet to help stretch the leather. Keep the shoes on until after they have cooled. Try your shoes on without the socks and if they are still too tight, repeat the process.

466. Ditch the k-cups. If you love your Keurig, as we do, you can purchase a reusable cup for under nine dollars.

467. Don't buy breakfast on the way to work. It is much cheaper and faster to buy pre- made breakfast sandwiches or burritos and heat one up before you leave.

468. Even cheaper than purchasing frozen breakfast sandwiches or burritos is to make your own and freeze them. Burritos with eggs and cheese and chopped meat can be rolled, cooled and frozen. You can also do this with a toasted English muffin, cheese, egg and your favorite meat.

469. If you're going to buy a home, save a minimum of 20% down so you don't have to purchase private mortgage insurance (PMI).

470. Stop prescreened offers of credit and insurance for 5 years by opting out at www.optoutprescreen.com or calling 1-800-567-8688.

471. Visit littlefreelibrary.org to find free small libraries where the books are free.

472. Take the time to teach yourself about the basics of investing through library books, YouTube videos, or blogs; there are so many to choose from.

473. Visit Khan Academy for free SAT prep. You can even link your Khan account to your College Board account to get automated recommendations based on your PSAT results.

474. There are many variables to consider when purchasing a vehicle including insurance and repair costs; overall dependability, NHTSA safety ratings, and theft frequency of the model; as well as the individual vehicle's history reports if buying used. Make sure to research all of these before making your decision.

475. Put a few grains of rice in the bottom of your salt and sugar

shakers; this will keep the salt or sugar from clumping so you won't be tempted to just throw it out, avoiding waste.

476. If purchasing spices in bulk make sure they are whole spices, instead of ground. Whole spices can be stored in the freezer for up to three years.

477. If you bake a lot of cupcakes or muffins, it will save you money in the long run to purchase silicone muffin pans since you won't need to buy disposable cupcake liners.

478. Rather than buying prepared vegetables such as lettuce, carrots, or celery, save money by purchasing whole veggies and washing and cutting them yourself.

479. Rather than buying compostable seed starting pots, start your seeds In cardboard egg cartons.

480. Keep your kitchen sink as free of dishes and your counters as clutter free as possible. A messy kitchen can kill your desire to cook, which may tempt you to spend more

481. Replace the switch for your bathroom fan with a timer switch. The exhaust fan certainly plays an important role in your

home by venting excess moisture to the outside, but leaving it on longer than necessary wastes electricity directly and works against your HVAC by wasting the air you're paying to heat or cool.

482. Don't throw that stale bread out. You can use it to make bread crumbs, stuffing , croutons, French toast and many other recipes.

483. Take advantage of dual-credit courses where available. Many high schools now offer courses with college credit within the school, which is a great way to save money on future education expenses. If your local high school doesn't offer such classes on campus, students may – with permission – be able to take a course for dual credit at a local college.

484. If you have sold a vehicle, make sure you get a refund of your remaining registration fee from the state.

485. Make sure to register new purchases for warranty purposes. While there is usually still a registration card, most major manufacturers offer registration via E-mail or text. Be sure to keep a copy of the paper card or the electronic confirmation of registration. While the manufacturer warranty is generally in-force even without registration, a benefit of registering is that you will often be contacted directly if there is a product recall.

Note that the demographic info sometimes requested during registration such as yearly income and your age is not required.

486. If you receive class action law suit notices in the mail, be sure to read them carefully. Registration for follow-up notices, class inclusion, and/or award payout is usually very easy and is often done online. If you are a valid member of the class, this can often be an easy way to ensure you get your fair share of any settlement or judgment.

487. Cut your pet's nails yourself. Invest in a good pair of nail trimmers and save a lot of money over the pet's life.

488. If your financial institution offers and online bill pay feature, take advantage of it. Not only will you save on stamps and paper checks, you can schedule recurring payments to streamline management of your home finances.

489. Do you have gift cards to places you won't go? You can sell them through cardpool.com or re-gift them to someone who could enjoy the card.

490. Do you have single earrings, broken jewelry, or jewelry you simply no longer want? Sell it. Gold and silver jewelry can be sold easily at many pawn shops and most jewelry stores.

491. Does your company offer referral bonuses? If you refer someone, make sure you understand the terms of the bonus, especially what your referral must do when applying to be sure you are eligible for the bonus.

492. If you are one who enjoys reading, you can get paid to write book reviews. Check out the following websites:

- onlinebookclub.org
- https://www.wcwonline.org/Women-s-Review-of-Books/writing-for-womens-review-of-books
- https://www.booklistonline.com/writing-for-booklist
- http://www.theusreview.com/USRcontact.html
- https://www.kirkusreviews.com/about/careers/

Each company has different requirements so be sure to read their instructions carefully.

493. Diaper wipes and/or wet wipe boxes are great for automobile first aid kits, a child's tackle box, portable art kit, even travel snack boxes. They are also great to store small toys such as jacks, marbles and Legos.

494. Create your own snack mix from leftovers. Keep all the leftovers from cereals and snacks and put them into an airtight

container. Once you have approximately 6 cups of snacks, make sure they are all in bite size pieces. Place the snack pieces in a bowl, add 5 Tablespoons of melted butter, plus 1/2 - 1 teaspoon of your favorite spices such as garlic powder, onion powder, or nutritional yeast, and 2 Tablespoons of Worcestershire sauce. Completely mix and bake at 225 stirring every 15 minutes for approximately 1 hour. Let cool completely and store in airtight container.

495. Turn your skills into money in the gig economy. There are many services that have demand just about everywhere such as teaching music lessons, teaching English, shoveling snow, auto repair, tutoring, house cleaning, leaf raking, mowing yards, house painting, moving furniture and other stuff, bartending for special occasions, housesitting, pet sitting, dog walking, babysitting, driving for Lyft or Uber, home repairs, running errands, assembling furniture, housecleaning and delivering food. You can list the services you perform on sites like craigslist.org or Handy.com.

496. If you have a lot of scrap metal around your home, you may be able to sell it to a local recycling or salvage company. Call in to find out what materials they will buy, how much they currently pay, and what requirements or restrictions they might have.

497. You can wad mesh produce bags and use them in place of plastic scouring pads to take care of tough to clean spots on your

dishes, pots, and pans.

498. Work as an at-home call center employee. There are many companies that hire at-home employees including 1-800-Flowers, Amazon, American Express, American Airlines, the Newton Group, Teleflora, and U-Haul just to name a few. Many companies have geographic restrictions and internet or other requirements.

499. Take online surveys at MySurvey, Vinedale Research, Survey Junkie, iSay, Inbox Dollars, Pinecone Research, Harris Poll Online, Global Test Market, and many others.

500. Get paid to do research at home through https://askwonder.com/researcher/signup

501. Now the really hard part, go out and do what needs to be done. Pick something you can do today to save or make money and get started. Thinking about making changes is easy, action is the hard part. You've got this!

www.ingramcontent.com/pod-product-compliance
Lightning Source LLC
Chambersburg PA
CBHW021443210526
45463CB00002B/621